easy GUITAR play along

CHRISTMAS Songs

PLAY 8 SONGS WITH TAB AND SOUND-ALIKE CD TRACKS

ISBN 978-1-4768-1264-9

HAL•LEONARD®
CORPORATION
7777 W. BLUEMOUND RD. P.O. BOX 13819 MILWAUKEE, WI 53213

Visit Hal Leonard Online at
www.halleonard.com

Have Yourself a Merry Little Christmas

from MEET ME IN ST. LOUIS
Words and Music by Hugh Martin and Ralph Blane

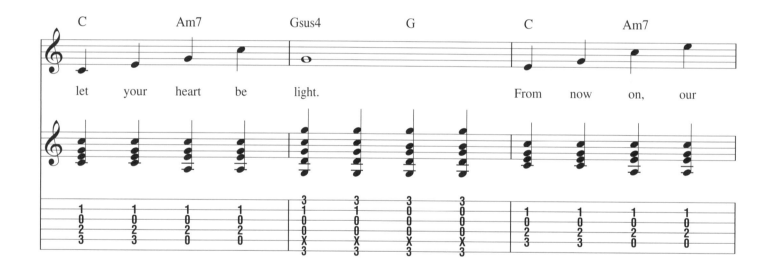

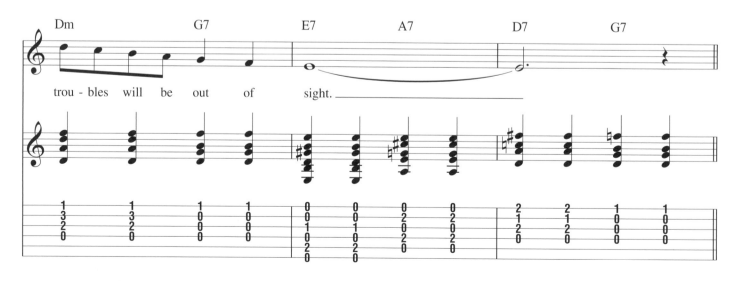

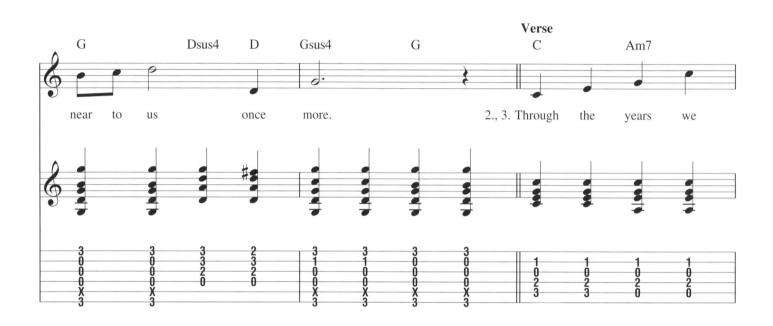

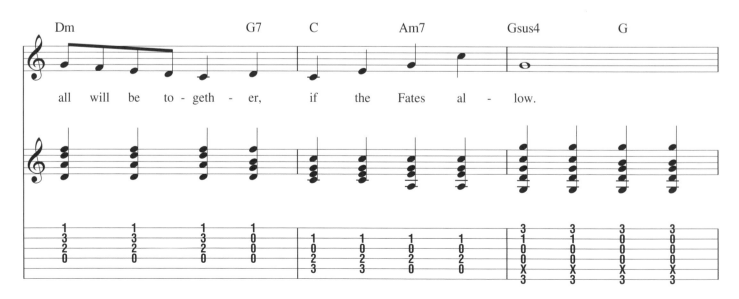

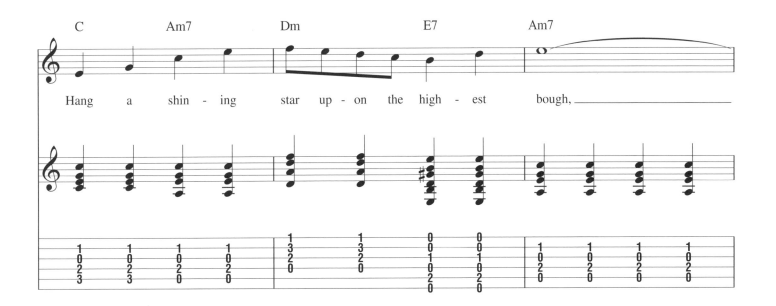

Hang a shin - ing star up - on the high - est bough, _____

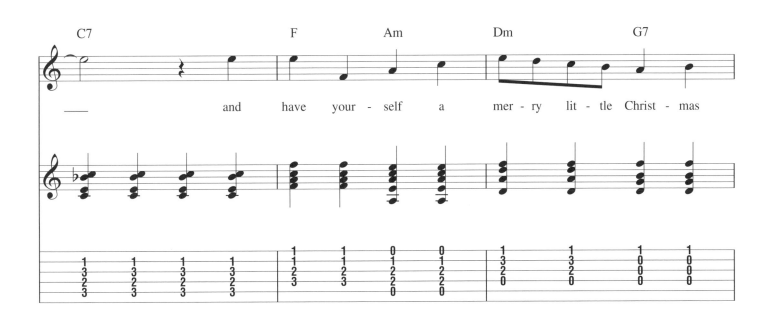

_____ and have your - self a mer - ry lit - tle Christ - mas

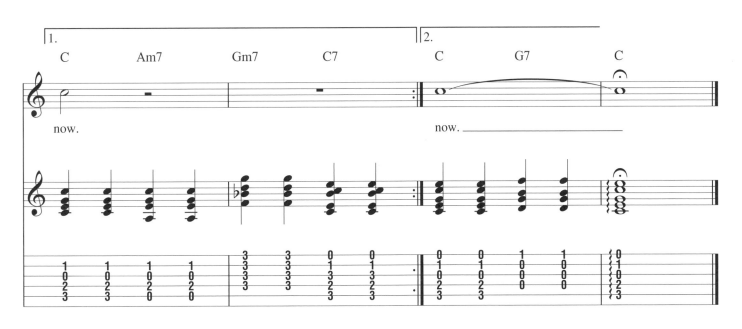

now.

now. _____

A Holly Jolly Christmas

Music and Lyrics by Johnny Marks

Run Rudolph Run

Music and Lyrics by Johnny Marks and Marvin Brodie

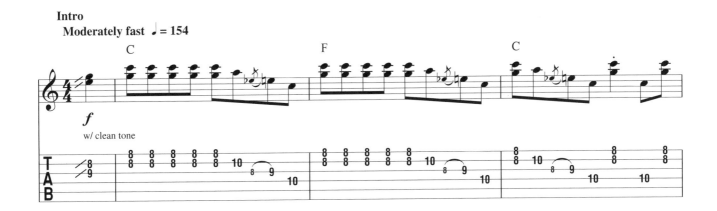

Out of all the rein - deers, you know you're the mas - ter - mind.

Run, — run, Ru - dolph,

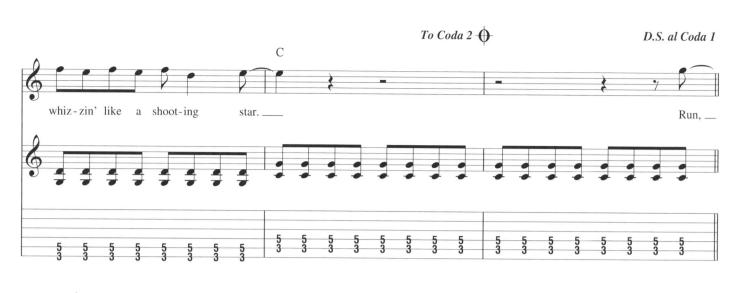

whiz - zin' like   a   shoot-ing   star. ___   Run, ___

⊕ **Coda 1**

Guitar Solo

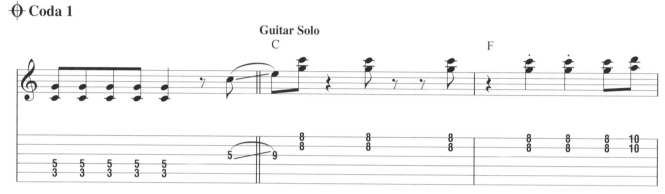

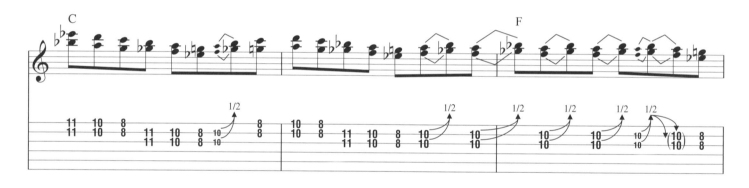

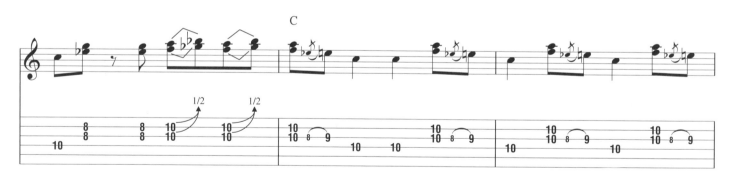

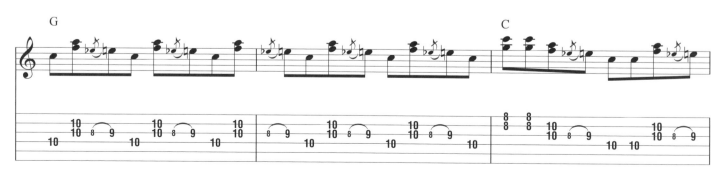

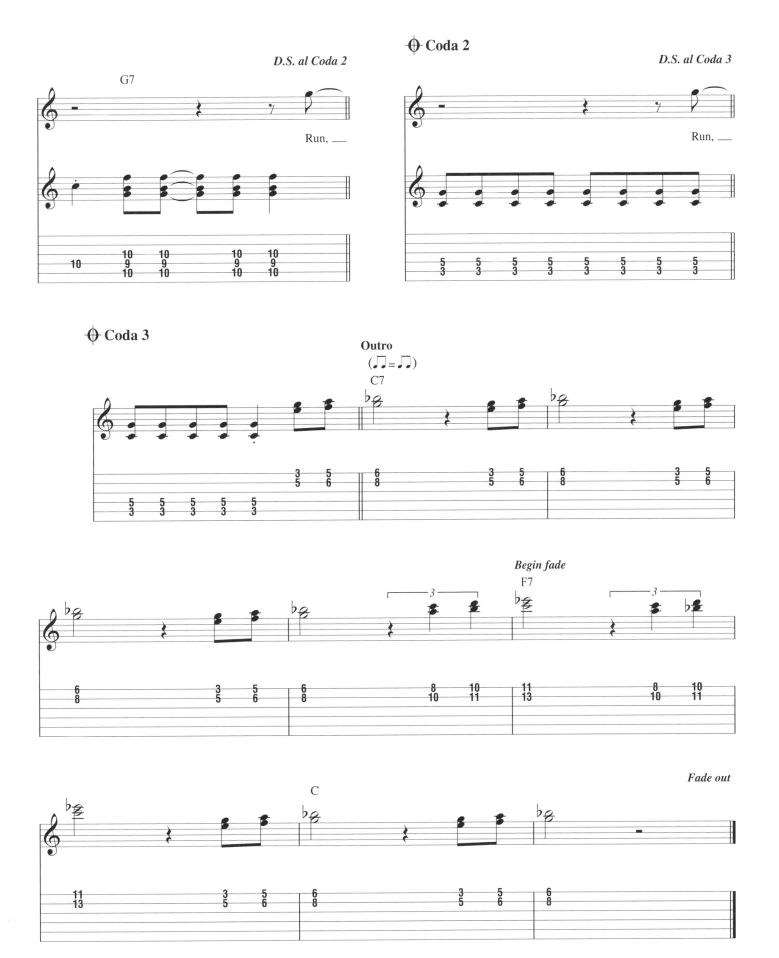

Additional Lyrics

2. Said Santa to a girl, "Child, what would please you most to get?"
   "A little baby doll that can cry, sleep, drink and wet."
   And then away went Rudolph, whizzin' like a Saber jet.

The Little Drummer Boy

Words and Music by Harry Simeone, Henry Onorati and Katherine Davis

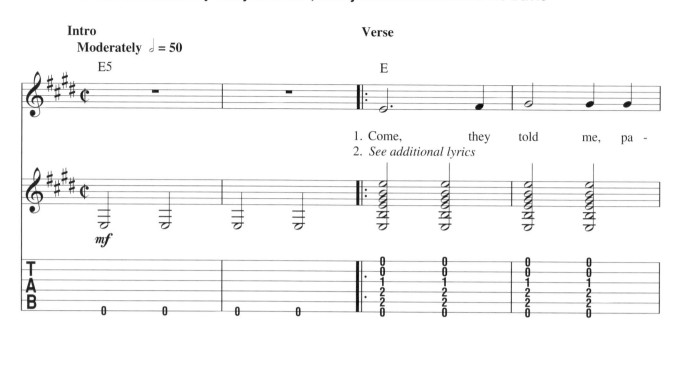

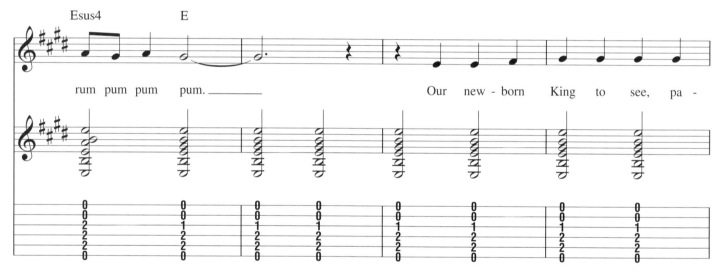

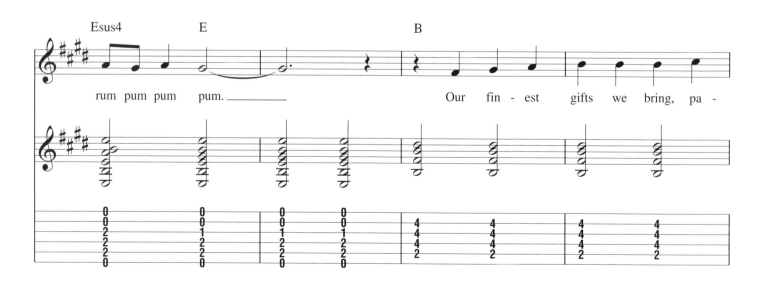

Additional Lyrics

2. Baby Jesu, pa-rum pum pum pum.
   I am a poor boy, too, pa-rum pum pum pum.
   I have no gift to bring, pa-rum pum pum pum,
   That's fit to give our King, pa-rum pum pum pum.
   Rum pum pum pum, rum pum pum pum.
   Shall I play for you, pa-rum pum pum pum, on my drum.

Santa Claus Is Comin' to Town

Words by Haven Gillespie
Music by J. Fred Coots

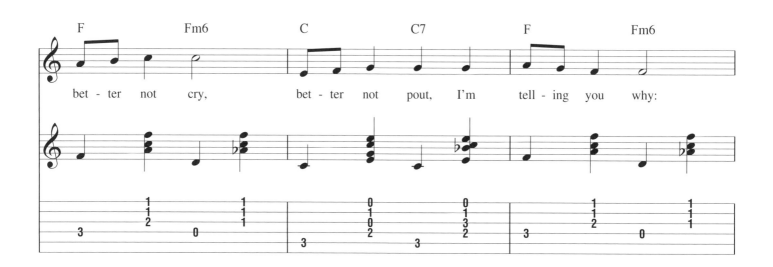

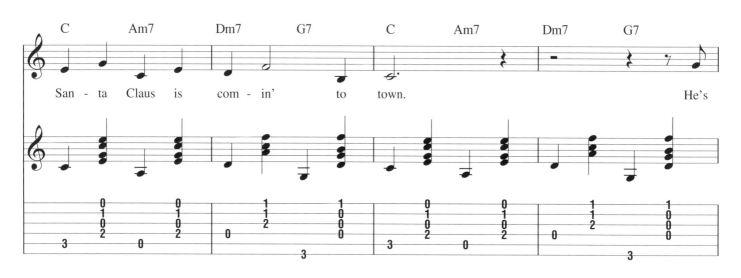

Sleigh Ride

Music by Leroy Anderson
Words by Mitchell Parish

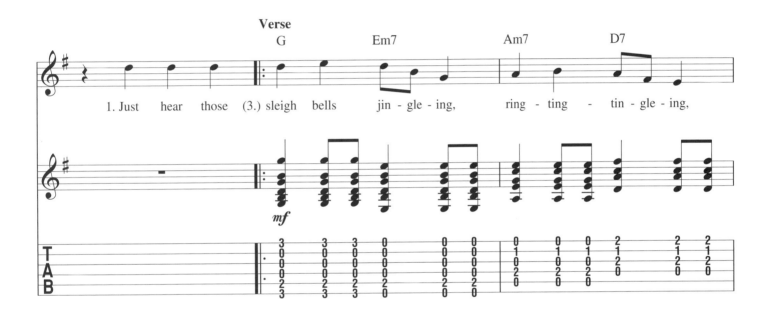

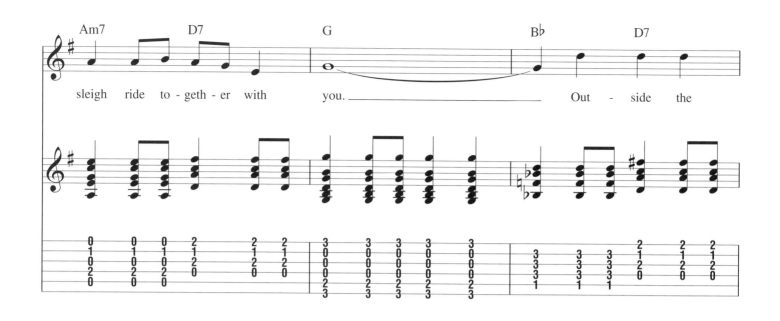

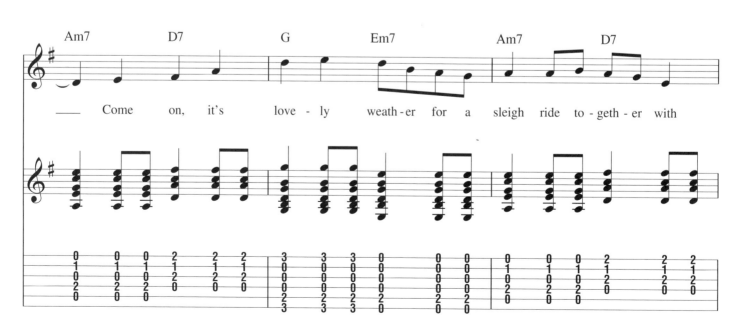

Silver and Gold

Music and Lyrics by Johnny Marks

Winter Wonderland

Words by Dick Smith
Music by Felix Bernard

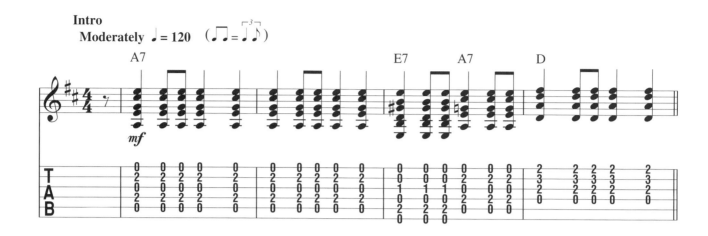

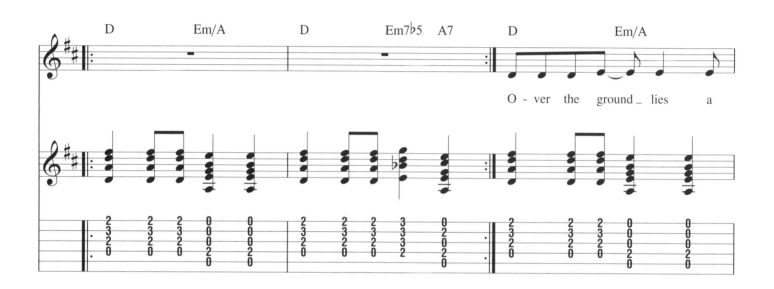

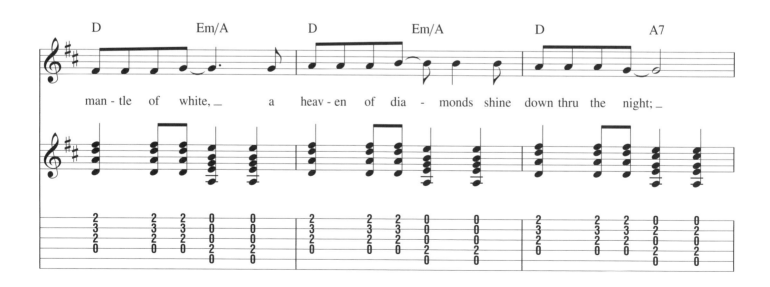

Additional Lyrics

Bridge In the meadow we can build a snowman,
And pretend that he's a circus clown;
We'll have lots of fun with Mister Snowman,
Until the other kiddies knock him down!

4. When it snows, ain't it thrillin',
Though your nose gets a chillin'.
We'll frolic and play the Eskimo way,
Walkin' in a winter wonderland!